Stay Encouraged

"Hear my cry, O God;
listen to my prayer.
From the ends of the earth I call to you,
I call as my heart grows faint;
lead me to the rock that is higher than I."

Psalm 61:1–2, NIV

STAY
Encouraged

K.P. Yohannan

BOOKS

a division of Gospel for Asia

www.gfa.org

Stay Encouraged

ISBN 978-1-59589-030-6

Published by gfa books, a division of Gospel for Asia
1800 Golden Trail Court, Carrollton, TX 75010 USA
phone: (972) 300-7777
fax: (972) 300-7778

Printed in the United States

For information about other materials, visit our website:
www.gfa.org.

09   10   11   12   /   6   5   4   3   2

Table of Contents

Introduction

———

Every time I ran into him, I found him to be optimistic, smiling and full of enthusiasm. But a few months ago, I found him kind of down and out, his eyes no longer bright, the smile missing.

Over a cup of tea, we began to talk about the struggles he had been going through. During this conversation, he looked up with tired eyes and simply said, "I just need some encouragement."

I was surprised and thought it odd to hear these words from his mouth. He is a Christian leader, responsible for hundreds of pastors and workers under his leadership, and here he was being so vulnerable, admitting his need for someone to come alongside him and lift him up.

You may be in that same place today. You may not have said out loud, "I just need some encouragement," yet in a thousand other ways you have "said" it—that look of despair and sadness, the sighing, the questions asked, the frowned face, drooping shoulders, pleading eyes.

If truth were known, you are craving some kind of encouragement . . . looking for it, longing for it and grieving because you have not found it.

Where are you? Hibernating? In the valley of discouragement? Is a heavy, dark cloud covering you? Do you wish to quit and run away from life itself?

I have been there.

The painful shadows of hopelessness and discouragement have often stretched across my path. There are times I have wished to get off from this fast-moving train of life. Many times I have said, "This is enough. I can't handle it anymore." I have shouted in silence, alone in the crowd.

But I want to assure you; you are not alone in the struggle. Jesus understands.

He experienced the awful, bitter waters of being tempted to remain discouraged. Hebrews 4:15 reminds us that "we do not have a High Priest who cannot sympathize with our weaknesses, but was in all points tempted as we are."

Take courage. The Lord will lift you up. He has done it for me a thousand times. No pit is so deep that He cannot reach you. No valley too bleak that He cannot escort you out. No night so dark that His light cannot penetrate.

There is hope.

You are important to the Lord. He made you and cares about you deeply. The pages of this booklet are His way of reaching out to you today.

CHAPTER ONE

It's Not Unusual

———

How are you?
At this moment, how are you doing? Perhaps you are on the mountaintop . . . or maybe you're camping out in the valley? Or maybe someone you know is going through a tough time.

I think it is safe to say that discouragement comes to the best of us. One of the most difficult things in life is to *stay* encouraged. The stuff that keeps us going continually leaks out. It seems we are so fragile, prone to live by our feelings and emotions, so easily discouraged.

Think about it. It really doesn't take much at all to get discouraged. It can be one look or one word, someone's silence, a telephone that doesn't ring or something we expected that didn't happen. The smallest thing can trigger discouragement. Even our own imaginations, which may have no concrete basis, can trigger its downward spiral.

Where does it come from? Sometimes it feels like ice cold wind that makes us shiver deep within, and like dominoes, all hope tumbles down and we land in the pit of despair, stripped of all joy and hope and feeling so helpless. There may be a thousand reasons for discouragement, but one thing is for sure: There is someone behind this sinister force. Our enemy: Satan.

His Most Subtle Tool

It was advertised that the devil was going to put his tools up for sale. On the date of the sale the tools were placed for public inspection, each being marked with its sale price. There were a treacherous lot of implements. Hatred, Envy, Jealousy, Doubt, Lying, Pride, and so on. Laid apart from the rest of the pile was a harmless-looking tool, well-worn and priced very high.

"The name of the tool?" asked one of the purchasers.

"Oh," said the adversary, "that's Discouragement."

"Why have you priced it so high?"

"Because it's more useful to me than the others. I can pry open and get inside a person's heart with that one, when I cannot get near him with other tools. Now once I get inside, I can make him do what I choose. It's a badly worn tool, because I use it on almost everyone since few people know it belongs to me."

The devil's price for Discouragement was so high, he never sold it. It's still his major tool, and he still uses it on God's people today.[1]

I know far too well just how often the adversary uses this tool. For the past 19 years, I have been doing a daily radio broadcast in India in my native language of Malayalam, a language spoken by 38 million people. In a given year, anywhere from 80,000 to 100,000 letters are received from those who listen to the broadcast.

Nearly 75 percent of these letters consist of people sharing the difficulties they are facing, their agony, disillusionment and hopelessness. They write in requesting prayer for these things. Yet what is alarming is that on a daily basis, an average of 25 letters come with the news of someone contemplating suicide, yet the person will wait until hearing back from me before going through with it.

Of course, a response is quickly sent and our staff prays. By the grace of God, only one person who had written in has actually committed suicide; all the others responded to the help given them in Christ's name.

This epidemic of the soul is not just one found in India, but all over our world. Discouragement knows no boundaries, whether rich or poor, educated or illiterate. We as human beings, no matter what caste, creed, culture or nation we come from, all face struggles in life.

I remember when I first began to realize this. It was in Singapore in 1971, when I attended an international Christian leaders meeting. The guest speaker shared how he recently suffered from a mental breakdown and ended up in the hospital for treatment. When I heard that, I was shocked! I couldn't fathom it. I could not understand how a preacher, an ordained minister serving God, could have had a mental breakdown. It didn't fit into my theology at the time. But as I grew in the Lord, I came to realize that this was not an uncommon thing. Discouragement and depression happen to a lot of godly people.

No matter how high a mountaintop experience we may have had, no matter how many revelations we may have received, no matter how many times the Lord has stepped in to rescue us before, we remain weak and fragile human beings.

No amount of gifting by the Holy Spirit or being baptized in the Holy Spirit, no amount of casting out demons or performing miracles, no amount of Bible knowledge or preaching will keep us from discouragement. It comes to the best of us.

Consider Jonah. Regarded as a prophet of God, he was sure to have heard God share some remarkable things with him. He experienced the Lord's grace and salvation from the belly of the fish. He saw how He lavished mercy rather than wrath upon the people of Nineveh. He saw God do incredible things in his day. Yet even after all of this, he became so discouraged that he prayed to die (see Jonah 4:3).

Or think about Elijah. This man of God experienced a miraculous victory on Mount Carmel, when fire fell from heaven and consumed a water-soaked sacrifice. He saw how the Lord glorified His name and destroyed all the prophets of Baal. When Elijah prayed, great things happened—a three-and-a-half-year drought ended in heavy rain.

But still, he experienced discouragement. First Kings 19:4 tells us that right after these incredible events, he "went a day's journey into the wilderness, and came and sat down under a broom tree. And he prayed that he might die, and said, 'It is enough! Now, Lord, take my life, for I am no better than my fathers!' "

Don't Pretend

There are many examples throughout the Bible of great men and women of God who experienced discouragement. The interesting thing is that they never tried to hide it. They told God about it. They came to the Lord with their feelings and discouragement.

So often we are tempted to cover up our discouragement because we don't want others to think we are weak. We don't want people to think of us as unspiritual. Yet when we read through the Psalms, we hear the desperate cries of many a discouraged man. Psalm 102:1–5 says,

> Hear my prayer, O Lord, and let my
> cry come to You. Do not hide Your
> face from me in the day of my trou-
> ble; incline Your ear to me; in the day
> that I call, answer me speedily. For my
> days are consumed like smoke, and
> my bones are burned like a hearth.
> My heart is stricken and withered like
> grass, so that I forget to eat my bread.
> Because of the sound of my groaning
> my bones cling to my skin.

The psalmist is discouraged. It is apparent that he is not trying to deny it or hide it from anyone.

And, as always, this honest approach to God brings refreshment and hope. This psalm ends with the writer crying out, "But You are the same, and Your years will have no end. The children of Your servants will continue, and their descendants will be established before You" (Psalm 102:27–28).

Most of all, Jesus did not hide His discouragement. In the Garden of Gethsemane we see Jesus, the One who was there at the spectacular creation of the universe, falling down on the ground in despair. In His moment of greatest need, He did not put on a show for His disciples but was honest and human before them.

> He took Peter, James and John along with him, and he began to be *deeply distressed* and *troubled*. "My soul is *overwhelmed with sorrow* to the point of death," he said to them. "Stay here and keep watch." Going a little farther, he *fell to the ground and prayed* (Mark 14:33–35, NIV, emphasis added).

Jesus is our perfect example in all things, even in how to handle discouragement. Although terribly burdened down by the events of the cross that soon faced Him, He was honest before His fellow man and before His Father.

Let us follow Him in this, and receive the invitation in all things to "humble your-selves, therefore, under God's mighty hand, that he may lift you up in due time. Cast all your anxiety on him because he cares for you" (1 Peter 5:6–7, NIV).

He has given us His promise that when we cry to Him, He will hear us. "The righ-teous cry out, and the LORD hears, and delivers them out of all their troubles. The LORD is near to those who have a broken heart, and saves such as have a contrite spir-it. Many are the afflictions of the righteous, but the LORD delivers him out of them all" (Psalm 34:17–19).

If you are one who is discouraged today, please, cry out to Him. His ear is tuned in to your cries, and He waits to be your help and comfort.

CHAPTER TWO

Divine Instrument

It seems that with all our knowledge, information and experience, we should be on top of the mountain more of the time.

I know this is how I often evaluate my life. I think that after all I've endured, I should now be able to face all kinds of problems without discouragement.

But it doesn't work like that.

I can preach a message and see hundreds of people set free. I can witness remarkable things that the Lord is doing in some of the most unreached parts of the world. But within a short time, I can find myself bogged down, discouraged and confused, wondering what to do next and trying to find a way to quit, slow down or find an easier path.

Finally, I realized that discouragement, although a tool of the enemy, is also an instrument of God, used to shape us and bring us into all that He has for us.

In his book *The Screwtape Letters,* C.S. Lewis gives the dialogue between senior devil, Screwtape, and the junior devil he is teaching, Wormwood. The instruction given to Wormwood on how to deal with man's disappointment and discouragement is eye-opening.

> Work hard, then, on the disappoint-
> ment or anti-climax which is certainly
> coming to the patient during his
> first few weeks as a churchman. The
> Enemy [God] allows this disappoint-
> ment to occur on the threshold of
> every human endeavor. . . . It occurs
> when lovers have got married and
> begin the real task of learning to live
> together. In every department of life
> it marks the transition from dream-
> ing aspiration to laborious doing.
> The Enemy takes this risk because He
> has a curious fantasy of making all
> these disgusting little human vermin
> into what He calls His "free" lovers
> and servants—"sons" is the word He
> uses. . . . Desiring their freedom, He
> therefore refuses to carry them, by
> their mere affections and habits, to

any of the goals which He sets before them: He leaves them to "do it on their own." And there lies our opportunity. But also, remember, there lies our danger. If once they get through this initial dryness successfully, they become much less dependent on emotion and therefore much harder to tempt.[1]

It's true. Take heart in the truth that God uses discouragement to work all sorts of good into our lives. By it, He strengthens weak knees, granting the fortitude to journey on and preparing us for the next seasons of life.

Discouragement also has a unique way of keeping us connected to Him. It is easy to forget how much we need God when the skies are blue, the sun is shining and the birds are singing. But watch the dark clouds roll in and the storms come, and we are forced to seek shelter—in Him. This is why the psalmist said, "But it is good for me to draw near to God" (Psalm 73:28). In another version this verse reads, "But as for me, the nearness of God is my good" (NASB).

Daily Drawing Near

In Exodus 16, we see a picture of how the Lord designed our spiritual lives. The Israelites were required to *daily* collect the manna

God provided for them. They couldn't collect enough on one day to last for two days, for if they collected more than they needed for that day, it spoiled and became full of worms. They couldn't store it up. What they gathered was enough to sustain them for *only one day.*

The Lord has designed our spiritual life like that as well. Daily we must come to Him to be refreshed and restored. Just like the Israelites needed to gather the manna daily, we need spiritual refilling daily.

And the beautiful thing is, He fills us whenever we come to Him. We are drawn to Him daily out of absolute necessity. Without Him we are like a branch cut off from the vine. It is good that we need to come daily to the Lord. If we didn't, we would so easily wander and try to live in our own strength. God loves us too much for that.

In Psalm 119:67 the writer tells us, "Before I was afflicted I went astray, but *now* I keep Your word" (emphasis added).

The affliction worked for good, drawing the psalmist back to keeping God's word. Our discouragement works for good in our lives as well, drawing us nearer to the Lord.

This also reminds me of the familiar verse, Romans 8:28—"All things work together for good to those who love God, to those who are the called according to His purpose."

God continually causes "all things" (and discouragement is one of the "things" included) to help us come back to Him continually for refilling. Truly, the nearness of God is our good.

I understand that it may be difficult to believe that God has a plan even in the discouragement you may be facing. But regardless, He can be believed. And He knows our breaking point (see Psalm 103:14). The struggles and all the difficulties you and I face are designed to reshape us, not to destroy us.

His Presence, Our Hope

Because we know that God is good and is able to work all things together for our good, we can find the strength of heart to continue on.

In 2 Corinthians 4:1, Paul says, "Therefore, since we have this ministry, as we have received mercy, we do not lose heart." If you read through 2 Corinthians, you'll soon find how it seems the whole book is filled with the struggles Paul faced. But underlying all of his struggles are the words, "we do not lose heart." You could write those words as the theme over every chapter in 2 Corinthians. It seems to be the declaration of Paul's life.

And because he took hope in the Lord, he did not lose heart. Why? Because it is not the absence of difficulties or the absence of problems that makes the difference. It is the presence of the Lord.

Paul was starving, shipwrecked, imprisoned, stoned, beaten and left for dead (see 2 Corinthians 11). He was on the verge of an emotional breakdown so that he almost lost his mind and "despaired even of life" (see 2 Corinthians 1:8). Paul's life was full of hardships.

But what made the difference was that Paul brought these hardships to God. He came to his Lord daily because in the pressures of the world and in the weakness of his flesh, he knew he could not stand alone. He focused on Christ, and it was Christ who caused him to stay in the fight and to stay encouraged.

This is why he was able to say and encourage others to "give thanks in all circumstances, for this is God's will for [us] in Christ Jesus" (1 Thessalonians 5:18, NIV). Paul knew from past experience the faithfulness of God to work good from each situation. His hope was in the Lord—not in his circumstances, not whether he had a good day or a bad one, not in being with the right people or difficult people.

In Genesis 37–39, we see this is the same way that Joseph lived. Although it seemed that time and time again things in his life just seemed to go wrong, we never hear Joseph complaining or grumbling. Why? Because of two reasons: First, he had faith in God—a faith that affected his perspective toward suffering. And the second reason is that God was with Joseph. All throughout the story of his life, we are told, "the LORD was with Joseph" (see Genesis 39:3, 21, 23).

The Power of Our Attitude

Paul and Joseph *chose* to put their hope in God. They could have easily stayed where they were at, in dismay over the troubles of their lives. But they did not do this. They lifted their eyes and put their hope in God.

Here is where we see how important our attitude is in every situation of life. Proverbs tells us that "[as a man] thinks in his heart, so is he" (Proverbs 23:7). This is the reason why Scripture also tells us to "watch over your heart with all diligence, for from it flow the springs of life" (Proverbs 4:23, NASB).

You see, our attitude is like a sail. Whichever direction we place our sail, those winds will take us to particular destinations. If we put our sail up to catch only the winds of discouragement and doubt, it is certain that we will reach the destination we set for. But if we choose to place our sail in the confidence of God's goodness, we are bound to be carried along by Him and see His faithfulness.

In his book *The Tale of the Tardy Oxcart*, Charles Swindoll writes about the importance of our attitude to all the situations of life.

> Words can never adequately convey the incredible impact of our attitude toward life. The longer I live the more convinced I become that life is 10 percent what happens to us and 90 percent how we respond to it. I believe the single most significant decision that I can make on a day-to-day basis is my choice of attitude. It is more important than my past, my education, my bankroll, my success or failures, fame or pain, what other people think of me or say about me, my circumstances, or my position. Attitude keeps me going or cripples my progress. . . . It alone fuels my fire or assaults my hope. When my attitude is right, there's no barrier too high, no valley too deep, no dream too extreme, no challenge too great for me.[2]

Our perspective is so very important. We can choose either to see these difficulties and become discouraged or to turn to our good Father and believe that He has a way to turn even the most difficult circumstances into good. It is the mystery of His sovereignty.

Flip through the pages of the Bible, and you will see, in story after story, how each person we revere as a hero of the faith encountered discouragement. Not one was exempt. And even the more modern-day faith examples had hills to climb and obstacles to overcome. Let us then, by faith, fix our eyes on the good that He will produce in our lives out of the difficulties that are bound to come, and stay encouraged because of Him.

May I take your hand and encourage you not to give up? Be strong on the inside.

CHAPTER THREE

Take Heart

Although God is able to take the plans of the enemy and use them for our good, we must also see these as the spiritual attacks that they are. Therefore, we must keep our mind and heart in gear, ready to stand against our adversary and receive the promises of God.

I want to share a few thoughts on things that have helped me in times of struggle and discouragement. God has given us focus in the battle and weapons to fight with.

First, no matter the reason for the discouragement, think about the Lord. Hebrews 12:1–3 says,

> Therefore we also, since we are surrounded by so great a cloud of

witnesses, let us lay aside every weight, and the sin which so easily ensnares us, and let us run with endurance the race that is set before us, *looking unto Jesus,* the author and finisher of our faith, who for the joy that was set before Him endured the cross, despising the shame, and has sat down at the right hand of the throne of God. For *consider Him* who endured such hostility from sinners against Himself, lest you become weary and discouraged in your souls.

It is when we look horizontally that we get discouraged. When we let what people say or think and the expectations people have of us to influence us, then discouragement sets in. When we look to men (horizontal) rather than to God (vertical), we easily become weary.

These verses say, "Look unto Jesus" and "consider Him." It is in bringing our lives before the Lord that we find encouragement. All our troubles and all our reasons for discouragement fade away when we look up and see Him.

When we do this, we realize that the difficulties we face are just another way for us to identify with His sufferings (see Philippians 3:10). He is able to turn them around into a means through which we become more Christlike. Discouragement simply becomes a way for His treasure to shine out through the broken clay vessels that we are (see 2 Corinthians 4:7). In our weakness, He is made strong. "Therefore I will boast all the more gladly about my weaknesses, so that Christ's power may rest on me" (2 Corinthians 12:9, NIV).

Second, think about the good things in life. Come before the Lord in praise. Philippians 4:8 tells us,

> Finally, brethren, whatever things are true, whatever things are noble, whatever things are just, whatever things are pure, whatever things are lovely, whatever things are of good report, if there is any virtue and if there is anything praiseworthy—meditate on these things.

Let us not make a list of all the reasons why we are in trouble or to stay discouraged. Don't think about the negative. Scripture says to think about things that are lovely and wholesome and of good report. Think on these things.

One of the reasons why people become cold and cynical is because they forget the place from where the Lord has brought them. They forget His goodness toward them in times past. They forget that He is faithful.

That is why throughout the Old Testament, God seemed to continually remind His people saying, "Don't forget. Celebrate the Passover year after year. This will remind you of Egypt and how I brought you out to freedom" (paraphrase, see Exodus 13:6–8). "Collect a jar of manna and save it to remember how I fed you in the wilderness" (paraphrase, see Exodus 16:32–33). "Take twelve stones out of the Jordan and make a place of remembrance. Then someday you can explain to others what I did for you" (paraphrase, see Joshua 4:5–7).

Likewise, we must keep ourselves in remembrance.

I encourage you to take some time now to write out a list of all the good things God has brought into your life. There are so many reasons to thank Him, and there is power and victory when we praise Him.

Consider this remarkable story of one man who chose to see the good things in his life rather than the bad.

As a recently retired man was sitting on his porch down in Kentucky, his Social Security check was delivered. He went to the mailbox to retrieve it and thought to himself, *Is this all my life is going to be from this time on? Just sitting on the porch waiting for my next Social Security check to arrive?* It was a discouraging thought.

So he took a legal pad and began to write down all the gifts, all the blessings, all the talents, and everything that he had going for him. He listed them all, even small things. For example, he included the fact that he was the only one in the world who knew his mother's recipe for fried chicken in which she used eleven different herbs and spices.

> He went down to the local restaurant, and asked if he could get a job cooking their chicken. Very soon the chicken became the most popular item on the menu. He opened his own restaurant in Kentucky. Then he opened a string of restaurants and eventually sold the Kentucky Fried Chicken franchise to a national organization for millions of dollars. He became their public representative and continued in that role until his death.[1]

Third, pray. Come before the Lord in prayer. You do not have because you do not ask. You do not find because you do not seek. The door doesn't open because you don't knock (see Matthew 7:7–8). Please pray. God really answers prayer. Please believe me. He does! It is a great encouragement to see God work in answer to prayer.

Remember 1 Thessalonians 5:16–18: "Rejoice always, pray without ceasing, in everything give thanks; for this is the will of God in Christ Jesus for you."

When we pray, our attitude is transformed. It is through prayer that the Lord changes our hearts and His peace is able to enter in, lifting us above the circumstances we may be facing.

Fourth, remember the Lord has good plans for you. He is faithful to you no matter what. We must remind ourselves of this truth continually, especially when things become difficult and unclear. Remind yourself and say, "God loves me. He called me for a purpose. He is always good, always faithful. I can trust Him." It is because of the assurance of who He is that we are able to continue on, never turning back or walking away from Him.

Fifth, live by faith, not by sight or feelings. Faith, by nature, is based upon what we cannot see. Things happen and we can't understand why. But we can *believe* that God will work it out for the best. We can cling to Him in depression, hurt or sorrow, knowing that these things are for a reason and that

He is strong enough to carry us through.

Only by faith can we look to the Lord in every situation. We may not know the solution yet, but He can give us peace as we trust Him to work all things together for our good. By faith we come to Him with whatever life brings—joys and sorrows—knowing that He is "our refuge and strength, a very present help in trouble" (Psalm 46:1).

Listen to this cry of faith in Habakkuk 3:17–19:

> Though the fig tree may not blossom,
> Nor fruit be on the vines;
> Though the labor of the olive may fail,
> And the fields yield no food;
> Though the flock may be cut off from the fold,
> And there be no herd in the stalls—
> Yet I will rejoice in the LORD,
> I will joy in the God of my salvation.
> The LORD God is my strength;
> He will make my feet like deer's feet,
> And He will make me walk on my high hills.

Sixth, know that no matter what, you are forgiven. Sometimes that is the hardest thing to believe. All the sins you have ever committed, all the sins you are committing now and all the sins you will ever commit until the last second of your life are forgiven. They have all been taken care of. All you need to do is acknowledge that work of God and live by it. Don't hold things against yourself. Live with forgiveness for yourself and others on a constant basis. Because of the blood of Jesus, we can "come boldly to the throne of grace, that we may obtain mercy and find grace to help in time of need" (Hebrews 4:16).

Finally, have patience with yourself. Philippians 1:6 says, *"Being confident of this very thing, that He who has begun a good work in you will complete it until the day of Jesus Christ"* (emphasis added).

Sometimes we get so discouraged and so impatient with ourselves. We can't see any good fruit being produced in our lives, and it tempts us to just give up. But we must remember that it takes time to be molded into the image of Christ.

Godliness, maturity and spiritual depth do not come through reading books and acquiring information. Often our problem is that we know so much. We know *about* what it means to be a good husband, a good father and a hard worker in the ministry. We know *about* being burdened by the Lord and about humility and brokenness. I know so many things in my head, yet still I long in many areas of my life to be the message I am preaching.

Rather, it is *God* working in us that brings maturity. The problem is in here, on the inside. I need to let the Lord work on me. I cannot do it, but God has a plan and a perfect way. *He* is the potter; I am the clay. With this understanding, I don't have to get all bent out of shape and be unforgiving with myself. I can know the Lord is working with me.

Keep in mind how Jesus responded to Peter after he denied Him. Jesus did not focus on Peter's mistake, but He saw beyond that, knowing what He was going to make him. Jesus was patient with Peter.

And just as God has patience with us, we must have patience with ourselves. We need to be objective and honest about our real condition, dismal as it may be. Yet we also must be willing to live with that truth and accept God's grace to change us instead of trying to correct ourselves (see Isaiah 45:9).

CHAPTER FOUR

Be an Encourager

—

Spread love everywhere you go: first
of all in your own house. Give love
to your children, to your wife or husband, to a next door neighbor. . . . Let
no one ever come to you without leav-
ing better and happier. Be the living
expression of God's kindness; kindness in your face, kindness in your
eyes, kindness in your smile, kindness
in your warm greeting.[1]

Take a minute and look around you. Look
close at the faces of people and see in
their eyes the desperate longing for understanding and their cry for a few words of
encouragement. If nothing else, just a look,
a pat on the back or a smile can make the

greatest difference in their day.

We are such self-centered creatures that from the moment we wake up until the moment we lay our head back on the pillow, we are consumed with ourselves. We think about *our* sorrow, *our* concern and *our* need for understanding and affirmation.

But what does the Bible say about this? "Give, and it shall be given unto you" (Luke 6:38).

Are you one looking for encouragement and appreciation? Then I have a suggestion for you: Encourage someone around you. Give to them what you are looking to receive, and you will be surprised how it will return back to you a hundredfold.

Listen to the words of Christ, "So in everything, do to others what you would have them do to you" (Matthew 7:12, NIV).

William Barclay once said, "One of the highest of human duties is the duty of encouragement. . . . It is easy to laugh at man's ideals. It is easy to pour cold water on the enthusiasm. It is easy to discourage others. The world is full of discouragers. We have a Christian duty to encourage one another. Many a time a word of praise or thanks or appreciation or cheer has kept a man on his feet. Blessed is the man who speaks such a word."[2] How true this is.

While reading through the well-known and loved book *Chicken Soup for the Soul*, I came across this story, which again shows the significant impact a little encouragement can have on the people in our lives.

A college professor had his sociology class go into the Baltimore slums to get case histories of 200 young boys. They were asked to write an evaluation of each boy's future. In every case the students wrote, "He hasn't got a chance." Twenty-five years later another sociology professor came across the earlier study. He had his students follow up on the project to see what had happened to these boys. With the exception of 20 boys who had moved away or died, the students learned that 176 of the remaining 180 had achieved more than ordinary success as lawyers, doctors and businessmen.

The professor was astounded and decided to pursue the matter further. Fortunately, all the men were in the area and he was able to ask each one, "How do you account for your success?" In each case the reply came with feeling, "There was a teacher."

The teacher was still alive, so he sought her out and asked the old but still alert lady what magic formula she had used to pull these boys out of the slums into successful achievement.

The teacher's eyes sparkled and her lips broke into a gentle smile. "It's really simple," she said. "I loved those boys."[3]

If we as parents or friends want to motivate our family members or people around us, we must be encouragers. We must choose to give sincere appreciation and honest praise for even the slightest good that people do. Thus we can spur others to greater achievements in life.

The renowned psychologist and thinker, professor William James of Harvard, mentions that each individual has tremendous energy, power, strength and potential in themselves. According to him, compared with what we ought to be, we are only half awake. We are making use of only a small part of our physical and mental resources. Stating the thing broadly, the human individual thus lives far within his limits. He possesses powers of various sorts that he habitually fails to use.

Encouragement is a powerful force. An earlier study shows that no one can achieve significant heights in life alone; it is always done with the help and assistance of others. In this, encouragement is without any doubt one of the most powerful things we can do to help others. Those who have studied the lives of people such as Charles Dickens or H.G. Wells know how timely a word of encouragement and praise proved to be the turning point in their lives, enabling them to attain great heights.

Consider Charles Dickens. His life did not exactly provide him with the conditions to be one of the greatest literary writers, yet that is what he became. Forced to quit school when he was 12 due to his father's imprisonment (for outrageous debt), Dickens spent his days pasting labels on bottles in a rat-infested workplace.

He desired to write and pursued that dream, only to have his work rejected time and time again. But one day, one of his stories, although denied for publication, was returned to him with a note saying that he was a great writer and the world needed him. These small words of encouragement sent Dickens running up and down the streets of London rejoicing. They also served as the staying power in his writing, therefore bringing us such literature masterpieces as *Oliver Twist*, *Great Expectations*, *The Tale of Two Cities* and others.

When you read about the lives of great men and women in history, you will always find there was some person or group who encouraged them, being the key factor to all that they achieved.

Just think about it. Who taught Martin Luther his theology and inspired his translation of the New Testament? Who was the individual who witnessed to Sadhu Sundar Singh of India? Who encouraged Mother Teresa to leave her home in Albania and travel to India? Who was behind the staying power of Amy Carmichael in the midst of endless years of physical suffering and difficulties on the mission field in India? Who was the elderly woman who prayed for years and witnessed to George Verwer for over a decade? Who financed William Carey's travel to India and his ministry?

You see, it is easy to understand. It doesn't take superstars and the most brilliant to encourage others. You can do it. I can do it. English poet, William Wordsworth, once said, "That best portion of a good man's life, his little, nameless, unremembered acts of kindness and love."[4]

I want to ask you, when was the last time you encouraged someone with your words or actions? We are most Christlike when we can show compassion and love for others. Jesus always affirmed and strengthened the weak, the lonely and the unwanted.

One of the most significant ways in which we can encourage others is to listen with our hearts to what they are saying. Often people say things not in words, but in their feelings, their actions and even their silence. While listening, ask the Lord to give you understanding to what they are saying. Then you will be able to respond with the determination to encourage and strengthen them.

There are times you can do things to show your support and encouragement. Sometimes it is sharing finances, giving them a book that will help them through a difficult time or sharing a song that will encourage their heart. It could be just simply taking the time to sit down and listen to them.

Daily look for something positive and encouraging that you can do or say to the people around you to strengthen them in this life's journey. Appreciate people and acknowledge even the little things that they do. Never underestimate the power of positive words and a solid handshake or pat on the back.

When I look back over the years of my serving the Lord, there have been numerous times of deep discouragement and struggles. Many times I have thought about running away from it all. In each of those times, it was some brother or sister saying "I am praying for you" or doing something to encourage me with their words or actions that gave me the courage to continue the journey. Even today that is true.

May you be that to someone today. "Give, and it will be given to you: good measure, pressed down, shaken together, and running over will be put into your bosom. For with the same measure that you use, it will be measured back to you" (Luke 6:38).

Concluding Remarks

Please, my precious brothers and sisters, when discouragement comes, look to the Lord. Use every hard situation, every bad circumstance, every illness—everything—as an opportunity to seek the Lord and rely on Him.

When you are discouraged, I strongly encourage you to remember the promises of God, given to us in the Bible. Many times it has helped me to say these promises out loud, applying their truths to the situations I am facing at that time. Boldly confess that:

- God is a good God. He is my Father (see Romans 8:15).
- The Father loves me the same as He loves Jesus (see John 17:23).

- I am redeemed by the blood of the Lamb by grace . . . a new creation (see Revelation 5:9, 2 Corinthians 5:17).

- God is the strength of my life (see Psalm 27:1).

- I can do all things through Christ . . . (see Philippians 4:13).

- The Lord is my Shepherd. I want nothing (see Psalm 23:1).

- Surely He has born my sickness and carried my sorrows, and by His stripes I am healed (see Isaiah 53:5).

- My God shall supply all my needs according to His riches (see Philippians 4:19).

- I can resist the devil, and he will flee from me (see James 4:7).

- No weapon formed against me will prosper (see Isaiah 54:17).

- I am more than a conqueror through Jesus Christ (see Romans 8:37).

- All things work together for my good (see Romans 8:28).

- I am bold as a lion (see Proverbs 28:1).

- He will never leave me nor forsake me (see Hebrews 13:5).

- Blessed be the Lord, who daily loads me with benefits (see Psalm 68:19).

- As the days, so shall my strength be (see Deuteronomy 33:25).

- When I am weak, then I am strong (see 2 Corinthians 12:10).

- Let the weak say I am strong (see Joel 3:10), for the Lord is the strength of my life.

God's faithfulness and His mercies are new every morning! God wants us to know this. It is beautiful to know the freshness of God and how He restores our souls. Stay encouraged!

If this booklet has been a blessing to you, I would really like to hear from you. You may write to Gospel for Asia, 1800 Golden Trail Court, Carrollton, TX 75010. Or send an email to kp@gfa.org.

Notes

Chapter 1

[1] Charles R. Swindoll, *The Tale of the Tardy Oxcart* (Nashville, TN: W Publishing Group, 1998), p. 164.

Chapter 2

[1] C.S. Lewis, *The Quotable Lewis*, ed. Wayne Martindale and Jerry Root (Wheaton, IL: Tyndale House Publishers, Inc., 1989), p. 161.

[2] Swindoll, *The Tale of the Tardy Oxcart*, p. 38.

Chapter 3

[1] Swindoll, *The Tale of the Tardy Oxcart*, pp. 163–164.

Chapter 4

[1] Jack Canfield and Mark Victor Hansen, *Chicken Soup for the Soul* (Deerfield Beach, FL: Health Communications, Inc., 1993), p. 3.

Stay Encouraged

2 William Barclay, *Letter to the Hebrews: The Daily Study Bible* (Edinburgh, Scotland: St. Andrews Press, 1955), pp. 137–138.

3 Canfield and Hansen, *Chicken Soup for the Soul*, pp. 3–4.

4 Jack Canfield and Mark Victor Hansen, *A 2nd Helping of Chicken Soup for the Soul* (Deerfield Beach, FL: Health Communications, Inc., 1995), p. 3.

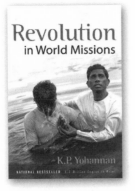

Instill
. . . a passion for the lost.

Impart
. . . fresh zeal for New Testament living.

Stamp
. . . eternity on your eyes.

If you've been blessed by the insight K.P. Yohannan has shared through this booklet, you will want to read *Revolution in World Missions*, his first and most popular book.

When We Have Failed—What Next?

The best *is* yet to come. Do you find that hard to believe? If failure has clouded your vision to see God's redemptive power, this booklet is for you. God's ability to work out His best plan for your life remains. Believe it. (88 pages)

Order online at www.gfa.org
or call 1-800-WIN-ASIA
in Canada 1-888-WIN-ASIA

Booklets by K.P. Yohannan

A Life of Balance
Remember learning how to ride a bike? It was all a matter of balance. The same is true for our lives. Learn how to develop that balance, which will keep your life and ministry healthy and honoring God. (80 pages)

Dependence upon the Lord
Don't build in vain. Learn how to daily depend upon the Lord—whether in the impossible or the possible—and see your life bear lasting fruit. (48 pages)

Journey with Jesus
Take this invitation to walk the roads of life intimately with the Lord Jesus. Stand with the disciples and learn from Jesus' example of love, humility, power and surrender. (56 pages)

Learning to Pray
Whether you realize it or not, your prayers change things. Be hindered no longer as K.P. Yohannan shares how you can grow in your daily prayer life. See for yourself how God still does the impossible through prayer. (64 pages)

Living by Faith, Not by Sight
The promises of God are still true today: *"Anything is possible to him who believes!"* This balanced teaching will remind you of the power of God and encourage you to step out in childlike faith. (56 pages)

Principles in Maintaining a Godly Organization
Remember the "good old days" in your ministry? This booklet provides a biblical basis for maintaining that vibrancy and commitment that accompany any new move of God. (48 pages)

Seeing Him
Do you often live just day-to-day, going through the routine of life? We so easily lose sight of Him who is our everything. Through this booklet, let the Lord Jesus restore your heart and eyes to see Him again. (48 pages)

Stay Encouraged
How are you doing? Discouragement can sneak in quickly and subtly, through even the smallest things. Learn how to stay encouraged in every season of life, no matter what the circumstances may be. (56 pages)

That They All May Be One
In this booklet, K.P. Yohannan opens up his heart and shares from past struggles and real-life examples on how to maintain unity with those in our lives. A must read! (56 pages)

The Beauty of Christ through Brokenness
We were made in the image of Christ that we may reflect all that He is to the hurting world around us. Rise above the things that hinder you from doing this, and see how your life can display His beauty, power and love. (72 pages)

The Lord's Work Done in the Lord's Way
Tired? Burned out? Weary? The Lord's work done in His way will never destroy you. Learn what it means to minister unto Him and keep the holy love for Him burning strong even in the midst of intense ministry. A must-read for every believer! (72 pages)

The Way of True Blessing
What does God value most? Find out in this booklet as K.P. Yohannan reveals truths from the life of Abraham, an ordinary man who became the friend of God. (56 pages)

When We Have Failed—What Next?
The best *is* yet to come. Do you find that hard to believe? If failure has clouded your vision to see God's redemptive power, this booklet is for you. God's ability to work out His best plan for your life remains. Believe it. (88 pages)

Order booklets through:
Gospel for Asia, 1800 Golden Trail Court, Carrollton, TX 75010
Toll free: 1-800-WIN-ASIA
Online: www.gfa.org